LEARNING CENTERS
in the Classroom

Learning Centers

IN THE CLASSROOM

Jimmy E. Nations, Editor

National Education Association
Washington, D.C.

Acknowledgments

The major part of this report was written by Dorothy Neubauer under a contract to the Department of Curriculum and Instruction of the Montgomery County (Maryland) Public Schools (MCPS). Though the material was written by Ms. Neubauer, the ideas came from numerous teachers, teacher specialists, and supervisors who participated in conferences and workshops on the topic and who reviewed written materials and gave suggestions for revisions.

Jimmy E. Nations, a former assistant director in the Department of Curriculum and Instruction of MCPS, gave leadership throughout the development and preparation of the materials and edited the final report.

The learning centers were developed by teachers, principals, and parents who participated in an in-service course taught by Betty Holden, a classroom teacher in MCPS, with assistance from Mr. Nations. Although some of the learning centers have been revised and adapted to provide continuity and consistency, credit for the original conception and design goes to the following:

"Take a Closer Look"	Harriet Murphy
"Everything Is Beautiful"	Ann Hannapel
"Adjective Alley"	Martha Beshers
"What Time Is It?"	Annalee Brooks
"Seeing China"	Ronald Webb
"Our Mathematics Laboratory"	Margaret Goins
"Everyday Economics"	Eleanor Curd

The manuscript was reviewed by Billie Breaux, 2nd grade teacher, Indianapolis (Indiana) Public Schools; and by Evelyne J. Hardiman, 6th grade teacher, Phoenix (Arizona) Public Schools.

Copyright © 1976
National Education Association of the United States
Stock No. 1802-8-00

Library of Congress Cataloging in Publication Data

Main entry under title:

Learning centers in the classroom.

Bibliography: p.
1. Open plan schools. I. Nations, Jimmy E.
LB1029.06L43   371.3   75-35986
ISBN 0-8106-1802-8

4/20/78 Bakers Tcyler 3.50

CONTENTS

1. Purpose of Learning Centers

1. Purpose of Learning Centers

"Is this what you want?"

"Is this the way you want me to do it?"

"What should I do now? I've finished the arithmetic problems."

"Why do we always have to read whenever we have any free time? I'd rather make something."

If you're hearing questions and comments such as these, day after day and from most of your students, don't just answer the questions; consider what the questions may be telling you.

They may be telling you that the students in your care see learning as "doing what teacher tells you to do." They may be telling you that you are limiting their access to different ways of learning, to different ways of using their time. They may be telling you to re-examine your teaching to see how successful you really are in attaining one of the most important goals for all students: the development of the desire and ability to learn independently.

There arc a number of teaching-learning techniques that can be used effectively to help students develop the skills of independent learning. One is the learning center, and there is a great variety of

learning centers to be found in our schools. The centers vary in subject, size, and organization. Some examples of actual learning centers have been included in Chapter 3 to show their broad scope and
versatility. Learning centers can range in subject from telling time
to human relations, and can be constructed for a single purpose for
one day only or for an ongoing semester's project. Whatever the
type, a learning center will always use a wide variety of means to
display its subject—pictures, music, words, objects to handle, etc.
No two learning centers are exactly alike in appearance, because
they reflect the work of different teachers and students and their
specific needs.

All learning centers, however, share a purpose: to help young
people develop independent learning skills. For this reason many
educators believe that learning centers can:

- Help students become self-motivated
- Help students learn at their individual paces
- Help students and their teachers know one another better as
  persons—not just as stereotyped "students to be taught" and
  "teacher who teach"
- Help students develop their own goals—sometimes with, sometimes without, the help of teachers and/or other students
- Provide opportunities for students to evaluate their own
  progress
- Help students learn how to work independently
- Provide opportunities for students to learn from one another—
  to give help and to receive it
- Provide opportunities for students to explore different ways of
  learning and to find the ways that work best for them. This
  should be a continuing exploration, with freedom and encouragement to try something again that wasn't successful the
  first time around
- Help students use different ways of communicating ideas, information, and feelings
- Help students become acquainted with various learning
  resources and learn how to use them
- Help students develop a multi-faceted approach to learning as
  they discover that there are many kinds of knowledge, skills,
  and ways of acquiring and using them
- Provide teachers with many opportunities for assessing needs
  and achievements of individuals and the group and for planning
  appropriate learning experiences; provide opportunities for
  students to participate in these activities.

The organization of learning centers varies from one situation to another. In schools that have a team-teaching organization, learning centers are planned and carried out on a team-wide basis. Still other schools use learning centers within a self-contained classroom.

Learning centers are planned and set up by teachers and students. Some of the centers provide learning experiences in which everyone is required to participate. Some provide learning experiences that are required for *some* students but are open to anyone who wishes to participate. Still other centers provide activities which are not assigned to all but are open to any interested student.

Whatever the subject, size, or organization of the learning centers, there are some characteristics that should be common to all of them:

1. They should look enticing so that they attract attention and interest.
2. They should include manipulative materials whenever possible and appropriate.
3. They should be set up so that students have no difficulty figuring out what they are to do. At the same time, they should be open-ended so that students can modify or add to the activities at the center.
4. They should be designed in such a way that learning opportunities can be extended and expanded by changing or adding materials and/or instructions. (One center, for example, can contain as many as four levels of learning and still deal with the same topic.)

Learning centers share these characteristics because they are all concerned with independent learning, a goal commonly accepted by educators. It crops up frequently in educational literature and in speeches at almost any educational conference. Stating goals and techniques is easy; however, achieving them is another matter.

We can begin by making sure we have a clear understanding of what independent learning is and what it looks like in the behavior of students. Unless we are clear about the goal itself and what it looks like when it is translated into human behavior, we can't be sure just what it is we are striving for, nor will we be able to determine whether progress is being made.

One caution: we say—and the words come easily; we've said them so often—our goal is to help students learn how to learn.

11

Learn how to learn *what?* Are the skills of independent learning the same for music, art, and literature as they are for science, mathematics, history, geography, and social problems? What are the common elements? (There are some.) Just as important, what are the differences? Dissecting a frog may well be a fine way to learn some of the skills a scientist needs. Dissecting a poem may kill a student's interest in literature and discourage the student from ever wanting to write—or read.

Learn to learn *what?* Keep this in mind as you look at the following statements of what students do or do not do—if they are independent learners or moving in that direction. The statements are admittedly generalized and need to be particularized by the teacher and each student, so that they are applicable to different areas of learning and to different skills of learning. Also, the statements, as written, represent what might be termed *mastery*. Students because of their youth haven't yet achieved mastery but are moving toward it—at least toward the best they can do. So you should look for signs that indicate students are moving ahead, making progress, and don't expect, for example, that every student will always know where to find the resources needed for solving a particular problem.

Now for the statements. They do not, obviously, include everything about independent learners. You may well want to add to the list yourself—and, especially, you will need to add to the refinements that adapt learning skills to a particular area of learning.

Students who are learning how to learn:

- Set goals for themselves—sometimes on their own, sometimes with help from others
- Decide what they need to do to achieve their goals
- Decide what resources they need
- Know where to find these resources and know how to use them
- Know when they need help from others—a teacher, another student, someone else
- Accept help from others, knowing that everyone can't always "do it alone," and knowing also that it is a strength, not a weakness, to accept help when help is needed
- Evaluate the progress they are making toward their goals, and use the results of their evaluations to help improve learning
- Re-evaluate their goals and change them when there is need for change. For example, students often set unrealistic goals for

themselves—usually too ambitious, but sometimes not challenging enough. Frustration, restlessness, and boredom are some of the consequences. They are indicators that students need to revise their goals; and to do this they should look at their original goals and achievements in relation to their new ones.

Students who are learning how to learn:

- Initiate projects on their own
- Experiment with different ways of working and learning, including working with others
- Explore new interests, new ideas, new areas of learning
- Have a reserve of things they want to do when they have completed a particular task.

Students who are learning how to learn:

- Don't need constant prodding from an adult
- Don't always expect someone else to tell them what to do
- Aren't passive and aren't always willing to accept what they read, see on TV, or hear from adults and their peers; they question and follow through on their questions
- Don't quit on the job; when they start something, they see it through—unless a mid-point evaluation indicates good reason for redirecting their energies.

The ways of teaching that lead to independent learning are interesting and challenging, but they are also demanding and time-consuming. Some teachers feel that it is easier to tell their students what to do than it is to involve them in directing their own learning. Likewise, many students feel that it is easier to do what they are told to do than it is to question and explore on their own. The teachers and students who feel this way may be right—and they may also be the ones who can scarcely wait for Friday to release them from the boredom of school.

Unfortunately, chances are very good that many students from do-as-I-tell-you settings will not acquire the skills of independent learning that can help them become continually interested and continually interesting human beings. Such students are more likely to become gullible consumers of highly advertised products, passive recipients of packaged entertainment, and sub-standard contributors to society. In the labor market, these passive qualities will make it easy for them to find little challenge on the job, to wait to be told what to do, and to need fairly constant supervision.

This may be overstating the case—a little, but not much. If students spend most of their early years in a setting that encourages them to expect others to tell them what to do and how to do it, they will not—at the age of 18 or 21 or 30—suddenly become self-motivated or self-directing. The skills of independent learning are skills that have to be learned. True, some students will acquire these skills even in a school setting that gives little encouragement to their efforts, but most students will need guidance and support. Learning centers are a way for teachers to offer this, and the individual learning that students gain is something they will find useful for the rest of their lives.

2. Establishing and Using Learning Centers

2. Establishing and Using Learning Centers

The Teacher

We have said rather explicitly that long exposure to the do-as-I-say method of teaching can inhibit students' independent learning. Is it inconsistent, then, to offer some learning center "how-to's" for teachers? Will the suggestions inhibit teachers' efforts to develop their own techniques? This could happen if there were a rigid set of how-to's, with no room for teachers to shop around and experiment. Most teachers, however, are interested in knowing what other teachers have tried, how it has worked, and what they would recommend to their colleagues on the basis of their own experience. Understandably the reactions of teachers who listen to or read about the work of another teacher are varied:

"It *might* work for me."

"It might work for me—with modifications."

"Never. Anyway, not with the students I have now."

"It sounds pretty good. But the principal would never approve."

"She must be teaching in an old ballroom! With our kind of space it would be chaos—sheer chaos."

"I wonder if the other sixth-grade teachers would be interested. I'd feel better about trying this idea if several of us were working together."

"I'm not going to wait for the rest of the teachers to get interested. I'll experiment on my own."

"Is it worth the effort? It would take an awful lot of time to get the students ready. And it would take a lot of time to collect the material."

"Maybe those bored teen-agers would really like this. Maybe they could 'do their thing' and stop complaining about not being able to."

"All those tape recorders and record players and projectors—who has that kind of equipment? And try to get it!"

"Maybe the parents in that community are different from ours. If we try to prepare our parents for something new, there's so much flack from the noisy ones that there's no chance of success. If we don't alert them to a proposed change, they complain because they weren't involved—even if the change seems to be working well for the kids."

"I'd like to know what happens when the newspapers get hold of what was going on in that school."

"If the principal really meant it when he said he would support judicious innovation, he ought to go along with *this*."

Whatever your reactions, and there are many possibilities, we hope you will find in this chapter some ideas about learning centers that will be of interest and value to you. Most of the ideas come from teachers. Most of them have been selected because they seem to be relevant for anyone using learning centers; some of them, however, are directed particularly to teachers using learning centers for the first time.

Getting Started

Maybe you didn't get organized to use learning centers early in the school year. So what's wrong with beginning in December, or February, or April? You will have known your students longer; you will know more about each one of them and how each one learns or doesn't learn. You may sense a certain restlessness that says: "We need a change. We're ready to try something different." Learning centers can be established any time you and the students are ready.

Part of the learning that comes from learning centers results from students' participation in planning and helping to set them up. Consider what students can do to collect materials and to help with the physical arrangement of the center, once its purpose and the plans for it are clearly understood. In the suggestions on the following pages, some of the opportunities for having students help are pointed out. There are many others that could have been mentioned, but space doesn't permit an exhaustive listing, and common sense tells us that a comprehensive listing isn't necessary anyway. For example, when you read, "Designate centers by attractive captions, display charts, posters, pictures," you know—because you know the individual student's competence and need for recognition—which ones can help collect pictures, which ones can make posters, and so on. If you are a teacher of very young children, you know the more limited range of their contributions and should proceed accordingly.

The kind of school organization within which you work will affect the way you use suggestions for planning and establishing learning centers. In a team-teaching situation, you will be working closely with other teachers. In a self-contained classroom, you will probably be more on your own. But your colleagues in other self-contained classrooms may also be using learning centers or may be interested in trying them. If so, the self-contained classroom can also open up many possibilities for working together to evaluate plans, ideas, techniques, and results. It also provides the possibility for using different classrooms for different learning centers. This has the dual advantage of increasing the number of possible centers and reducing the amount of space that has to be set aside for learning centers in any one classroom.

Specific How-To's

1. If you have decided to experiment with learning centers and this is your first experience with them—don't get in a big hurry. Begin the year with the kind of program you are accustomed to and feel comfortable with. Start making plans for learning centers; then, when you and the students are ready, begin making the centers part of the total program. Maybe you will start out with only one center and add others gradually as you and the class are ready. You may have done some planning before the opening of the school year, but you'll want to re-examine your plans and make some judgment as to whether they are appropriate for the group of students you have or whether they need minor—or drastic—modifications.

2. Find out as much as you can about your students. Observe; talk with them; examine permanent records—remember that no one source of information should be considered final. Evaluate your judgments in the light of what you learn from other teachers, but don't be hasty in disregarding

19

your own judgments if they fail to coincide with another teacher's opinion about any given student.

3. Study the curriculum. Consider how it relates to your students as you begin to know them. Establish some tentative goals—short-range and long-range—and make some decisions about the kinds of teaching techniques, including learning centers, that seem likely to be effective.

4. Study the physical setting to determine how it can be structured for the use of learning centers. What space is available, in your classroom or elsewhere in the building, and how can it be best used?

5. Visit other classrooms and schools with learning centers. It is helpful to see learning centers in operation at any level.

6. Read current literature on learning centers. (See the Annotated Bibliography on pg. 61.)

7. Before you start establishing a learning center, consider carefully what can probably be best achieved through total group instruction and what can probably be best achieved through learning centers. Arrive at a tentative plan for a program that includes some individual instruction, some small group instruction, some total group instruction. Make your plans specific enough to provide structure and guidance, but remember that you may want to modify the plan later and that you will need room for flexibility. Use centers part of the day or most of the day. Use them for some subjects or for all subjects, depending on the needs of the students and on your own teaching style. Have some centers that are required for all students; some that are required for specific individuals; some that are optional.

8. Before you begin using learning centers, find ways to inform parents about your plans. The success of any new learning technique can be jeopardized predictably by negative attitudes on the part of parents—attitudes that are more likely to develop if parents do not have an early opportunity to get accurate information about what is being planned and how it can affect their child's learning. "Guess what we did at school today!" followed by a child's enthusiastic version of "what we did" may be a fine follow-up to prior information, but it is not the most prudent way to introduce parents to learning centers.

Parental concern is legitimate and should be respected. Parental support is needed and should be cultivated. Parents should, therefore, have ample—and early—opportunity to discover what learning centers are, how they fit into the total instructional program, and what they can do to promote their child's learning.

There are many possible ways to provide information. Here are just two suggestions:

a. Send a brief description of your plans to parents. Invite them to come to a room meeting if they wish to find out more about how the learning centers will be used. For this meeting set up one or two sample centers so that parents can visualize what is intended and thereby be in a better position to ask intelligent questions about how such centers can help their children learn.

b. Talk with your principal and the PTA chairperson about the desirability of having one or more PTA meetings on the topic of learning centers. If such meetings are planned, again set up sample learning centers so that parents can see what they look like and be in a position to ask questions about how they will be used.

9. Understanding how to use the learning centers is most important; be sure you take plenty of time to help students learn how to make the best use of them. After you have made some judgments about the needs of your students, the goals it seems important for them to achieve, and the ways in which learning centers can help them achieve these goals and meet their needs, talk with your students about various plans. If they have been exposed to learning centers in other classrooms, they will already have some understanding of their operation and this understanding will be helpful to you. If learning centers are new to them, it will probably take longer to accustom themselves to the idea and to clarify their responsibilities and opportunities. Remember that your enthusiasm will be a prime factor in stimulating students' interest in using learning centers.

10. Expect students to want to move around and be prepared for the inevitable noise of busy activity. At the same time, work with students to establish routines that will help reduce the needless distractions that hamper good work at any point in the room. Establish routines for moving about, for determining the number of students to be at a center at any given time, and for handling equipment and materials.

11. Make your first learning center challenging, but make it

simple enough to avoid confusion and frustration. Encourage students to help in deciding on room arrangement. Ask them to help collect at least some of the needed materials.

12. Use as many sources as possible for collecting materials—other teachers, students, parents, the instructional materials center, and your own continuing accumulation of things that can be used for instructional purposes.

13. See that centers contain different kinds of learning materials and activities. Some learners have been frustrated and impeded in their learning by too much emphasis on reading and writing; give them an opportunity to learn through use of manipulative materials, too.

14. Make sure that the centers are attractive. This can be achieved by such things as eye-catching posters and interesting arrangements of learning materials. Students can help and will learn from the experience.

15. Provide for immediate feedback—by answer code, checklists, self-correcting puzzles, and the like—so that students can proceed independently.

16. Allow time in your schedule to check students' work frequently. This is by no means in conflict with your goal of helping them to learn how to work independently. As they move toward the attainment of this goal, students need the support of knowing that you are aware of their progress, are sensitive to the problems they may encounter, and are available for help. Parents, too, will be reassured to know that their children are not playing around on their own but are actually working purposefully under your supervision and guidance.

17. If students are to be operating tape recorders, record players, or viewers, be sure they understand how to operate and care for the equipment. Working with teachers from other classrooms, you might enlist the services of older students who understand the equipment and can help younger ones learn how to use it. Their helping becomes, in itself, a learning experience.

18. Introduce each new center to the total class.

19. Have a planning period with the whole class at the beginning of each day—at least when you first begin to use learning centers. At the planning session, write plans on the chalkboard; one of your students may do the writing. The

students should understand the objectives for the day's work and the plans as they affect the school day—when they will be involved in direct instruction, when they will be doing independent work in centers, what choices they have, and what you (and perhaps other teachers) will be doing to help them. There will be times when this planning period with the total group needs to be followed by individual or small group conferences. Planning with students is essential, and many teachers have each student write out a plan for the day or for a longer period.

20. Plan your day so that you have time to meet with individual students and with small groups.

21. Evaluation is essential—and this means evaluation of the centers, evaluation of the ways students are using them, and evaluation of the results from using them. Some teachers set aside 20 to 30 minutes at the end of each day for an evaluation session with students. Together they refer back to the plans made earlier, discuss what was learned, evaluate the way the class worked, and plan to make changes in the next day's procedure if changes seem desirable.

    Depending on the maturity of the students and the skills they develop for directing their own learning, this late-in-the-day evaluation period may also include plans for the next day's work. As students arrive at this point, there may be times when some will immediately go about their work when the next school day begins, leaving the teacher free to meet with other students who need help.

22. Stress the importance of what students can do to evaluate the effectiveness of the learning centers. Questions can provide guidelines for the evaluation process. Some possible questions are: What did you expect to learn through the center? Were the instructions clear to you? Were the materials appropriate? Could you work well on your own? Could you work well with the group? How did you spend your time? What have you learned? What did you enjoy the most? The least? What would help you to make better use of the learning center or centers? What would you like to bring to add to the center?

    At later sessions, students can be more analytical. They should be asking: "Why did this work?" "Why didn't it work?" "Should we continue this particular center?" "Should we change it?" "How?" Usually it is wise to keep the first evaluation questions simple, particularly for young students. Some students will begin to be analytical sooner than you expect. Try to find ways to use their contributions so that they will stay interested in their own work and also learn more by helping their classmates.

23. Planning and evaluating sessions should include discussion of the procedures that have been set up to facilitate working at the centers. However, as a day proceeds, there will be times when the teacher observes that the students are not clear on procedures and, as a result, are not doing their best work. When this happens, it may be wise to bring the class back together again to reconsider the routines to be observed, to make sure that the routines and the reasons for them are understood, and to make changes if needed.

24. As students participate in planning and evaluating the centers, it is practically certain that some will talk too much, some won't talk at all—or only with prodding from the teacher, many of them will not keep to a point, and so on. At least a few of the students will probably sense these difficulties themselves. But if this doesn't happen, you can help students become sensitive to their need for greater skills in participating in group discussions and group decision-making. Sometimes you can do this by raising a few questions: How long did it take us to arrive at this conclusion? Did everybody participate in the discussion? Did we spend so much time in our discussion that we lost time we might better have used for something else?

Now comes the time for considering how to improve the skills of group participation. You and the students may begin by identifying what contributes to a good discussion, what gets in the way, and what skills each one needs to be an effective participant. Next comes a decision about how these skills can be learned. One conclusion might be that a learning center for discussion skills could give students the chance to work in small groups. If so, here is an excellent opportunity for students to help develop the objectives and plans for such a center. The effectiveness of the center can later be evaluated by what happens when students work in small groups and what happens when they come together as a single group in their overall planning and evaluation sessions.

Deciding What's Best

As students become more independent in their learning, more capable of planning and directing their own learning activities, teachers can be more flexible and productive in the way they use their time. With students busy in the learning centers, teachers tend to become more free to work with small groups or to have conferences with individuals. It should be repeated, however, that teachers who use learning centers as a teaching technique do not give up total group instruction. They decide for their class what is best achieved by total group instruction and what is best achieved by students' working on their own—either individually or in small groups. Teachers use the learning center in a variety of ways according to the abilities and maturity of the student.

How a learning center is used also depends on the particular capabilities of the teacher. Some teachers have a teaching style that can be addressed to several ways of learning that learning centers provide, e.g., group and individual instruction; other teachers have a teaching style that is compatible with only some of these different ways of learning, e.g., small and large group instruction. What particular techniques to use are a personal decision for each teacher to make. Although the learning center is a bona fide teaching technique, it does not carry a guarantee of success. Its success ultimately depends on the expertise and judgment of the teacher.

3.   Examples for Study

3. Examples for Study

It's always easier to talk about good instructional techniques than it is to put them into practice. And so it is with learning centers. But once we are clear about what we want to achieve, the job of translating good ideas into sound practice is less awesome—especially with a little help from our friends.

The purpose of this chapter is to describe seven learning centers that have actually been used in classrooms. The number is limited and represents only a few of many possibilities. They were developed through an in-service course that was offered to teachers, principals, and parents in the Washington, D.C., metropolitan area. For three months the group met one evening per week for sessions that lasted two and one-half hours. The course was essentially not unlike hundreds of other in-service courses. There were lectures, films, and group discussions. The difference was that most of the teachers and principals attending had not previously used learning centers for instructional purposes. So they were learning together. Everyone in the course was required to set up a learning center in a classroom; to watch students use it; to talk with them about what was successful, what was unsuccessful, what they liked, and what they didn't like; and then, finally, to revise and extend the learning center.

The designers of the course were concerned by some of the erroneous and limited practices which they had seen in a few classrooms. That is, many of the so-called learning centers were nothing more than a single activity or exercise. Frequently, every student in the group was expected to go through every activity in the same way that every other student did. The most disturbing element was that these series of activities were often unrelated and did not fit together into a well-rounded, total learning experience.

The best feature of the in-service course was that each participant was assigned to a small discussion group (five or six people) of similar grade level and/or interest. In these discussion groups they talked about their learning centers, how they had used them, and what the students' responses had been. In other words, they had the time to think about, analyze, describe, and evaluate what they had done. Beyond that, their fellow group members asked questions for clarification and made suggestions for revisions and extensions. At the next class session, members described and evaluated the revisions and extensions that they had tried. In this way an ongoing process of generating ideas, trying them, and assessing their outcomes was established—with encouragement and support from fellow group members.

Some people tried many different learning centers in their classrooms; others tried only a few. Most of the learning centers were used for not more than a few weeks. However, one learning center lasted the duration of the course and incorporated so many activities that it eventually spread out of the classroom into the hallway and involved students from other classes who couldn't resist the enticements of its learning activities.

Many kinds of learning centers were developed. One of the principals in the group was concerned because her school had six brand-new microscopes that had never been used. She designed a learning center which would allow the older students in her school to learn how to use the microscopes independently. Another principal devised a center about China. The center was used to initiate a social studies unit. An experienced teacher of young students set up a learning center on telling time. Another teacher set up a learning center to give students practice in using math skills which they had already been taught. And one teacher built a learning center in economics which was for the enrichment of those who chose to use it. Other learning centers were developed by parents in the group. One such parent was enrolled in a teacher education program and was preparing for her student teaching. She developed a learning center to help students appreciate the differences in people and as a consequence, to accept and value their own individuality. Another parent made a learning center for teaching about adjectives.

The participants in the course came a long way toward gaining new ideas for making their own classroom instruction more meaningful, useful, and interesting. Most importantly, they were able to translate those ideas into practice.

Some of the following descriptions suggest how to vary the center so that it can be adapted to different ability or age levels. The illustrations should show you how some teachers translated their good ideas into practice and should help you to clarify and put your own ideas into practice. In using these particular learning centers, or any others, the individual teacher is the one who decides how best to make the learning center an effective learning technique in the classroom.

TAKE A CLOSER LOOK

Take a Closer Look

This learning center was designed to be used eventually by all students in the upper levels of an elementary school.

In one corner of the classroom a heavy cardboard divider was set up around a stand-up worktable; next to it was a file cabinet, a bookcase, a moveable cabinet, and one regular worktable. A second file cabinet was used for storage of equipment when the cabinet and worktable were being used for other purposes.

Commercially produced, enlarged photographs of common objects—blades of grass, grains of salt, the veins of a leaf, the head of an ant—were used to decorate the room divider.

Materials and Equipment

- Microscopes
- Slides
- Written and recorded directions for using the microscope
- Listening station
- Recorded history of the microscope
- Taped directions for making a microscope from a nail, thin wire, and a glass of water
- Materials for sketching appearances
- Paper and pencils for writing descriptions of appearances
- Reference library
- Materials for making slides
- Some "mystery" slides

Some Activities

1. *Can you identify the objects?*

   The name of each object pictured in the display was written on the back of the picture. As students began to use the microscopes, they made their own sketches which were added to the display and used as a part of this activity. Each of the "mystery" slides was numbered and students kept a list of their guesses as to what each was. A complete answer sheet was made available later.

2. *Can you describe a microscope?*

   Some students made scale drawings and wrote accompanying directions for using a microscope. One group of students tape-recorded a verbal description of a microscope and its operation.

3. *Why are microscopes important?*

   Using the reference library, students prepared reports on who uses microscopes and how they are important to their work.

4. *Who developed the microscope?*

   After listening to a recorded history of the microscope, students wrote a brief summary.

5. *Can you make your own slides?*

   Students brought materials and objects from home for making slides.

Evaluation

Guide questions for teacher observation:

- When given a choice, do students frequently, or even sometimes, choose to work with microscopes?
- Are all activities and materials used?
- Do students use the microscope correctly?

Students' work folders are kept in a drawer of the file cabinet and checked by the teacher periodically.

Extensions

Environmental education is a very natural follow-up to learning about microscopes. Begin with a study of the tiny animals that live in ponds and streams. Expand to other studies of ecology.

Seeing tiny things in different sizes can be used as a lead-in to the study of measurements. And then to learning more about the metric system. . . .

Everything Is Beautiful*

This center was set up at the beginning of the school year in a primary classroom to introduce students to the use of learning centers. As a total group, the class learned the song, "Everything Is Beautiful."

The teacher had chosen a few pictures of people—young, old, different races and nationalities—to begin the collage which was to decorate the border around the room divider on which the words of the song were displayed. Periodically, the class discussed the pictures of people which individual students had cut from old magazines or brought from home to add to the collage.

Students were encouraged to do self-portraits, tape record their voices, and write stories about themselves. The old trunk of "dress-up" clothes next to the full-length mirror helped to stimulate imagination about who they might grow up to be.

Materials and Equipment

- Song printed on a chart
- Stacks of old magazines
- Scissors, paste
- Easel and paints
- Dress-up clothes
- Full-length mirror
- Tape recorder
- Writing paper, pencils
- Art paper, crayons, felt markers, pastels.

*Words and Music by Ray Stevens
© 1970 AHAB MUSIC COMPANY, INC.

Some Activities

1. *Show us how you look. . . .*
   Students did self-portraits, using the mirror for occasional reference. Some were done on 12" x 18" art paper; others were life-sized. Some children needed help in getting started. For them, it was easier to begin with a paper plate for the basic shape of the face.
   A good addition to this center would be a Polaroid camera so that each student's self-portrait could be accompanied by a snapshot of the student.

2. *Tell us about yourself. . . .*
   Students wrote or tape-recorded stories about themselves to share with other class members. At a later stage the class was taught how to conduct interviews. Students prepared questions and tape-recorded their interviews of friends.

3. *When you grow up. . . .*
   Students wrote and illustrated stories about what they would like to be and do when they grow up.

Evaluation

Guide questions for teacher observation:

- Which students are self-confident enough to participate productively in the learning center?
- Which ones need help in getting started?
- Which ones need help in settling down to purposeful activity?

Students' pictures tell a lot about their general level of maturity and their perceptual abilities, as well as about the strength of their self-concept. Their stories, written and spoken, tell a lot about their abilities to organize and express ideas.

Extensions

A related activity for the total group would be a study of the self-portraits of famous artists. How did they see themselves? What did they most want to include in their portraits?

Numerous language arts activities could be built into the center. Stories could be written about the people in the collage. Stories could be read about people from all around the world. A very natural extension of the center is to move into the field of career education. . . .

Adjective Alley

This multi-sensory learning center grew from a single red tulip in a bud vase displayed in front of a black velvet drape.

All of the students in the class were expected to write adjectives that would describe what they saw, touched, heard, or smelled. They then checked the lists of describing words that others had used. If any of their adjectives were not on the list, they added them and wrote their name beside their addition. The challenge was to think up fancy adjectives that had not already been included in the lists.

The students then used their most descriptive adjectives in stories, poems, and titles for pictures.

Materials and Equipment

- A flower or any other beautiful object
- Tape recorder and tape of at least three very different musical selections
- Sealed shoe boxes with opening covered by a small curtain; each containing an object or objects selected to provide different tactile sensations
- Dark glass bottles—each containing a different substance with a distinctive smell, e.g., perfume, peppermint oil, cat food
- Written instructions for activities related to each set of materials
- Word lists within easy reach, with a cover for each
- Paper, pencils, paints, crayons.

Some Activities

1. *Describe what you see. . . .*

   Written instructions directed the students to write down at least four adjectives that described the flower. After checking the list, and making additions, they were to think of one other object which each of their adjectives could be used to describe and write that word beside the adjective. For example, if a child listed "vivid," she or he might write "vivid sunset."

2. *Describe what you touch. . . .*

   After following a procedure similar to the preceding one, it was suggested that students make "feel boxes" at home to add to the learning center. Also, they were invited to write descriptive sentences or paragraphs about the things they like to touch and about things they don't like to touch.

3. *Describe what you hear. . . .*

   Instructions for writing adjectives for the music were given, and paints and crayons were made available for making pictures of the sounds. It was suggested that they write a title for their picture. Of course, they were to include at least one of their adjectives in the title.

4. *Describe what you smell. . . .*

   Again the same initial procedures were used. Then each adjective was to be used in a sentence.

Evaluation

The lists of adjectives created in the center serve as one form of evaluation. Are they as extensive and complete as expected? Who made what contributions?

The best evaluation is to determine if the students now use more varied and appropriate describing words in their spoken and written language.

Extensions

The objects to see, touch, hear, and smell can be changed occasionally and the center can be used for as long as there is a need or interest. For example, strange and unusual sounds might be used on the tape in place of the music. A new list of adjectives would then have to be started, of course.

Numerous language activities could follow. Haiku and cinquian might be introduced.

Another direction for follow-up is to use the center to introduce a science unit on the senses of sight, touch, hearing, smell, and taste. . . .

What Time Is It?

Models of clocks, puzzles, books, and work sheets were organized into this learning center that not only gave young students a chance to practice telling time, but also helped them to relate daily routines to time. In addition, they had an opportunity to become familiar with the parts of a clock.

The teacher was surprised by the variety of clocks that she was able to collect from other teachers in her school. The children enjoyed the variety.

The background for the learning center was a regular display board with pockets holding materials for students to use. Students' drawings of daily routines, labeled with the appropriate time of the day, decorated the spaces around a large clockface.

Materials and Equipment

- Clock models (commercial)—some with visible gears and moveable hands.
- Clock puzzle
- Books about clocks and telling time
- Instruction cards for setting a clock
- Work sheets for making clockfaces
- Paper pliers, scissors, paste, hole puncher, paper fasteners
- Some blank teacher-made booklets.

Some Activities

1. *Can you set a clock?*
   Small cardboard clocks with moveable hands were available on the table. Practice cards were in a pocket on the display board. The cards read:

   These children go to school at nine o'clock.
   Can you set a clock for 9:00?
   What time do you come to school?
   Does your clock look like this?

   Other examples were:
   This family has dinner at six o'clock.
   This boy gets up at seven o'clock.

2. *Can you make a clock?*
   Paper plates and other materials for making clocks were provided. Mimeographed clockfaces were the same diameter as the plates.

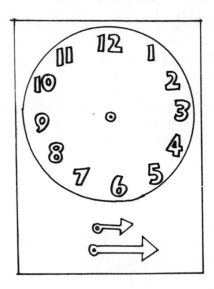

3. *Can you make a book?*

Blank books of manila art paper were in a pocket on the display board. Students used magazine pictures or drew pictures of their own to illustrate daily occurrences. Small clockfaces were then pasted at the bottom of each illustration and the hour and minute hands were drawn in.

Evaluation

Throughout the day the teacher checked to see which students could tell time by the hour, by the half-hour, and by five-minute intervals.

In small groups students were asked to set the clocks that they had made to a time designated by the teacher.

Extensions

Other types of clocks could be added to the center: egg timers, alarm clocks, etc.

An adventurous teacher might bring in old alarm clocks for the students to take apart and attempt to put back together.

A very natural extension of the center is to move into a study of calendars—another time-telling device.

Other mathematical experiences of counting and measuring could be added. . . .

Seeing China

The developing relationship between the United States and the People's Republic of China sparked the ideas for this learning center. A related—and for students, equally important—event was the arrival of two pandas at the zoo in Washington, D.C.

The major purpose of the learning center was to stimulate interest in three very different, yet closely related, areas of study. The center, therefore, combines activities in social studies, science, and mathematics. More in-depth study of China, unusual animals, and computers was to be done by the total class.

It is interesting to note that learning activities related to the study of China were consistently framed in a comparison with studies of our own country, thus providing more meaning for the children involved.

Materials and Equipment

- Filmstrip projector
- White window shade mounted to wall to be used as a screen
- Filmstrips on China
- Area, population, and resource maps of both mainland China and the United States
- Worksheets for comparing land areas, populations, and resources of the two countries
- Answer sheets to worksheets
- Class report list
- Pocket for work folders
- Instructions for some assigned tasks
- Two or three abacuses and small computers
- Written and recorded instructions for using the abacus and for using the computer
- Books, magazines, newspapers
- Large panda poster and magazine pictures of China.

49

Some Activities

1. *Filmstrips*
   After viewing and reviewing filmstrips, students made notes to be used in making an oral report to the class, preparing an outline, or writing a brief report.

2. *Worksheets*
   Using information gained from the maps, students completed worksheets comparing land areas, populations, and resources of China and the United States. Graphs (line, bar, and pie) were developed for presenting the comparative information.

3. *Speculation*
   A question was posed: "If you could develop a society using the best from the United States and China, what would it be like?"

4. *Research*
   Using magazines, newspapers, and books, students were challenged to answer a series of questions about the pandas Hsing-Hsing and Ling-Ling: "Where was I born? What do I eat? How far did I travel? Why am I important to the world?

5. *Computation*
   Learning how to use the abacus and the computer initiated a multitude of mathematical activities.

Evaluation

The major evaluation of the center was in the demonstration of student interests and the ideas sparked by various challenges and activities.

An opportunity was provided to assess students' understandings and misconceptions of both China and the United States.

An opportunity was also provided to assess students' ability to gather information from printed sources, filmstrips, photographs, and maps; and of their ability to report information in oral, written, and graphic form.

Obviously, students' ability to follow directions and their level of mathematical skills were overtly displayed and open to evaluation.

Extensions

This learning center was extended into three separate units of study and into three separate learning centers: one on China, one on unusual animals, and one on mathematical skills and understandings related to the operation and use of the abacus and the computer.

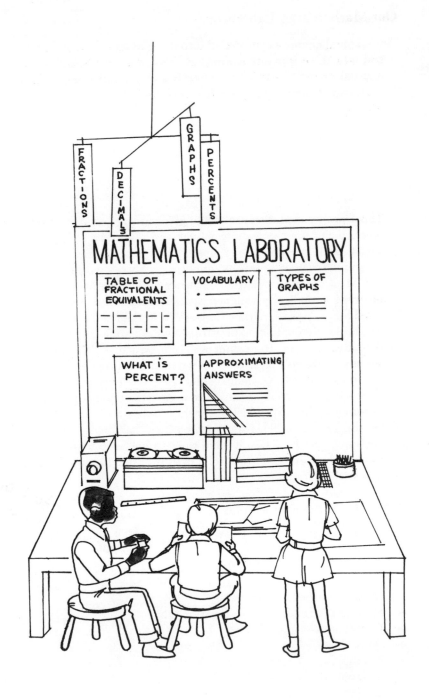

Our Mathematics Laboratory

This learning center was set up to give students an opportunity to practice and use the understandings and skills which they were acquiring from instructional groups in mathematics. Each student was required to spend at least 45 minutes each week working in this center. Most could choose from whatever activities were available. Some were periodically assigned specific tasks, and a few were assigned longer periods of time for working in the center.

In addition to containing filmstrips, manipulative activities, and mathematical games, the center was refurbished daily with extra copies of worksheets that had been used in instructional groups.

Not only did this learning center give students a chance to practice and reinforce their learnings, it gave the teacher a valuable opportunity to find out which students were, or were not, able to apply the understandings and skills which had been taught in instructional groups. Thus, it gave the teacher an opportunity to teach individual students and a solid basis for planning the specifics of successive instruction.

Materials and Equipment:

- Filmstrips on fractions, decimals, graphs, and percents
- Filmstrip viewer
- Taped explanations and instructions
- Tape recorder
- Games, manipulative materials
- Materials for making approximation table
- Dictionaries
- Work sheets
- Charts
- Assignment Sheets.

Some Activities

1. *Find the Definitions. . . .*
   A list of related mathematical terms was posted on a vocabulary chart. Students were instructed to use both the dictionaries and available mathematics textbooks to find their definitions.

2. *Fill in the Equivalents. . . .*
   Worksheets, with columns for percents, decimal fractions, and common fractions, were provided. For each example, only one column was filled in. The answer sheet had to be requested from the teacher.

3. *Compute the Batting Average. . . .*
   A list of players, times at bat, and number of hits was given. Students filled in the batting average for each player.

4. *Show It on a Graph. . . .*
   The sports section of the newspaper became a favorite source of data for graphs. Students were challenged to illustrate the same information with a line graph, a bar graph, and a pie graph.

5. *Approximate Answers. . . .*
   Instructions were given for constructing a table, using chart paper and a yardstick, for approximating answers to problems of percent.

Evaluation

The teacher observed students' abilities to use the skills incorporated in the center and supplemented those observations with exercises and written tests in instructional groups.

The results of observations and tests served as an impetus for revising the center and for revising small group instruction.

New assessments were then required, and an ongoing process of evaluation was established.

Extensions

This learning was kept up throughout the school year. However, it was constantly changing—in the same way that the specific topics of instruction in mathematics changed.

Everyday Economics

One of many learning centers set up in a single classroom, this one was not required of any student but was designed to help interested boys and girls learn to do comparative shopping; and to budget their money for a large purchase.

Most of the instructional materials were drawn from advertisements in newspapers, magazines, and catalogues—a very economical source!

The evaluation of the students' ability to budget their money was a long-term process. After planning a personal budget, they tried to live within it for several weeks. Like most adults, they revised their budgets a number of times before reaching workable ones. And, like most adults, they had to delay their large purchases longer than they wanted to.

Materials and Equipment

- Newspapers, magazines, catalogues
- Dittoed information sheets
- Sample spending plans (budgets)
- Worksheets for preparing a budget
- Different brands of various everyday products to be used for comparisons
- Paper, pencils, scissors, paste.

Some Activities:

1. *Compare!*
   Several students decided on large purchases which they would like to make, such as articles of clothing, records or a record player, or even a bicycle. They were encouraged to compare brands, models, and prices not only in the sources available in the learning center but also after school hours, in the local stores.

   A series of questions was posted on a bulletin board: Which paper towel absorbs the most water? How can you find out? Which gasoline gets the best mileage? How can you find out?

2. *Debate!*
   Two students who disagreed on the best bargain prepared a debate—with some help from the teacher. Their debate was presented before the entire class, following all the rules. Each had a time limit and each had an opportunity for a rebuttal. Other students voted on which was the most convincing argument.

3. *Advertise!*
   After doing a comparative study, a small group of students wrote a script and acted out television commercials for their favorite products.

   Some students wrote copy and made layouts for newspaper advertisements of their favorites.

4. *Budget!*
   Many students planned a budget identifying income from allowances, earnings, and gifts. They took careful note of every penny spent during the week and developed a plan for saving enough to make at least one significant purchase.

Evaluation

Guide questions:
° How much information did the students gather before assessing one item to be a better bargain than another?
° How sound is the logic of their arguments for preferring one product over another?
° Over a period of time, how many students are able to develop a workable personal budget?
° How many are actually able to make their large purchase—as a result of budgeting and saving?

Extensions

This learning center can gradually be extended to studies of paying cash versus using credit and to studies of savings accounts, banking and investments, and economic terms. With this background, the learning center could then be extended to studies of the free enterprise system, along with comparisons of various economic systems in the world.

Annotated Bibliography

Annotated Bibliography

There are numerous books with good suggestions of activities that might be built into learning centers. In the listing below we have included only books that are about learning centers, their uses, and how one can get started using them. All these references are paperbound.

Dean, Joan. *Room to Learn: Working Space, Language Arts, and a Place to Paint.* New York: Citation Press, 1974.

An excellent source of ideas for more efficient and creative uses of space, equipment, and materials. These helpful ideas are presented in attractive drawings accompanied by brief written descriptions.

Kaplan, Sandra Nina, and others. *Change for Children: Ideas and Activities for Individualizing Instruction.* Pacific Palisades, Calif.: Goodyear Publishing Co., Inc., 1972.

A very practical, step-by-step approach to helping teachers make the transition from knowing about individualized instruction to practicing individualized learning. Chapter 3 contains 21 ready-to-use learning centers.

Rapport, Virginia, editor. *Learning Centers: Children on Their Own.* Washington, D.C.: The Association for Childhood Education International, 1970.

A collection of articles by outstanding educators. Includes the following titles: "Personalized Teaching and Individualized Learning," "The Changing Role of the Teacher," "Organization for Individual Work," and "Children on Their Own—Centers and Stations for Learning."

Voight, Ralph Claude. *Invitation to Learning: The Learning Center Handbook*. Washington, D.C.: Acropolis Books, Ltd., 1971.

An easy-to-read, well-illustrated handbook that describes the concept of learning centers, gives realistic hints and tips for getting under way, presents student-tested learning centers, and reviews the most frequently asked questions about learning centers.

———. *Invitation to Learning 2: Center Teaching with Instructional Depth*. Washington, D.C.: Acropolis Books, Ltd., 1974.

Reviews basic concepts of center teaching, describes ways of recycling learning centers. Includes examples of learning centers for kindergarten, multi-skill learning centers, single-skill learning centers, and math centers.

Waynant, Louise F., and Wilson, Robert M. *Learning Centers: A Guide for Effective Use*. Paoli, Penn.: The Instructo Corp., 1974.

One of the more comprehensive and practical sources of information about learning centers. A well-written, semi-programmed book designed to answer such questions as: Why should I use learning centers? How can I get started? How do I evaluate student progress with centers?

Williams, Lois E. *Independent Learning . . . in the Elementary School Classroom*. Washington, D.C.: American Association of Elementary-Kindergarten-Nursery Educators, 1969.

The stated purpose of this book is " . . . to support teachers who are nurturing independence in their students and to encourage them to share their ideas and experiences with colleagues who are not involved in such projects . . . [to] stimulate discussion and argument, reading, experimentation, and action research projects."